Our Values

CELEBRATING DIFFERENT BELIEFS

By Steffi Cavell-Clarke

Crabtree Publishing Company

www.crabtreebooks.com

1-800-387-7650

Published in Canada
Crabtree Publishing
616 Welland Avenue
St. Catharines, ON
L2M 5V6

Published in the United States
Crabtree Publishing
PMB 59051
350 Fifth Ave, 59th Floor
New York, NY 10118

Published by Crabtree Publishing Company in 2017

First Published by Book Life in 2016
Copyright © 2017 Book Life

Author
Steffi Cavell-Clarke

Editors
Grace Jones
Janine Deschenes

Design
Natalie Carr

Proofreader
Crystal Sikkens

Production coordinator and
prepress technician (interior)
Margaret Amy Salter

Prepress technician (covers)
Ken Wright

Print coordinator
Katherine Berti

Photographs
nawawi/ Shutterstock: page 6
Other images by Shutterstock

Printed in Hong Kong/012017/BK20161024

Library and Archives Canada Cataloguing in Publication

Cavell-Clarke, Steffi, author
   Celebrating different beliefs / Steffi Cavell-Clarke.

(Our values)
Issued in print and electronic formats.
ISBN 978-0-7787-3261-7 (hardback).--ISBN 978-0-7787-3310-2
(paperback).--ISBN 978-1-4271-1892-9 (html)

    1. Religions--Juvenile literature. 2. Freedom of religion--
Juvenile literature. I. Title.

BL92.C38 2016   j200   C2016-906656-8
                                       C2016-906657-6

Library of Congress Cataloging-in-Publication Data

CIP available at Library of Congress

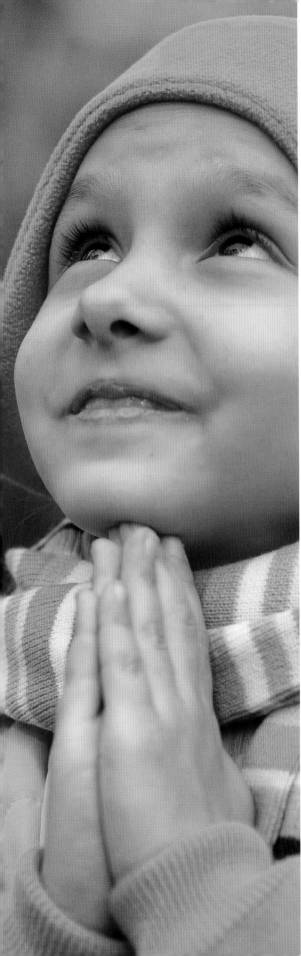

CONTENTS

Words that are bolded, like **this**, can be found in the glossary on page 24.

WHAT ARE VALUES?

Values are the things that you believe are important, such as telling the truth. The ways we think and behave depend on our values. Values teach us how we should **respect** each other and ourselves. Sharing the same values with others helps us work and live together in a **community**.

Respecting others

Working hard at school

Understanding different beliefs

Respecting the law

Values make our communities better places to live. Think about the values in your community. What is important to you and the people around you?

Helping others

Listening to others

WHAT IS RELIGION?

It is important to respect and celebrate other people's beliefs, such as their religion. Religions have values that people believe in, such as helping those who need it. To follow a religion is to **worship** and believe in something. Many religions have important places of worship, follow certain **traditions**, and hold **festivals**.

Kids celebrate Eid al-Fitr, a **Muslim** festival

There are also many people who do not follow a religion and choose to follow their personal values, or the things they believe in. We are all equal, no matter what we believe.

People who do not believe in a god or gods are called atheists.

WHY ARE BELIEFS IMPORTANT?

Our values are the things we believe in. Religion is one way that can help us decide which values we believe in. Our beliefs are important because they help us determine what is right and wrong

It is important to show respect and acceptance of other beliefs.

Our beliefs can help us be kind and caring toward others. They teach us to be respectful of other people's beliefs and religions. It is important to remember that we all have the **freedom** to believe in whatever we choose.

DIFFERENT RELIGIONS

There are many different types of religion that are practiced by people all around the world. Some of the religions with the most followers are **Christianity**, **Islam**, **Hinduism**, and **Judaism**.

I am a Christian. I follow Christianity.

I am Muslim. I follow Islam.

I am a Hindu. I follow Hinduism.

I am Jewish. I follow Judaism.

Michelle celebrates Christmas, a Christian festival.

Aaron celebrates Hanukkah, a Jewish festival.

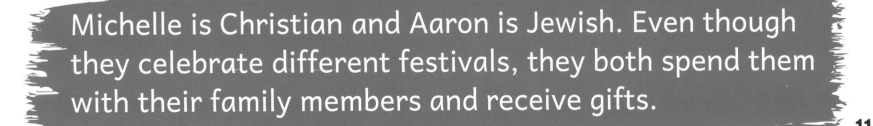

Michelle is Christian and Aaron is Jewish. Even though they celebrate different festivals, they both spend them with their family members and receive gifts.

RESPECTING OTHERS' BELIEFS

It is important that we respect other people's beliefs, even if we don't always understand what they believe. One way we can respect others' beliefs is by learning about and understanding other religions.

We can learn about different religions by asking questions. Abia follows Islam. Jordan is curious to learn more about Abia's beliefs. She asks Abia things such as where she goes to practice her religion.

"I go to a **mosque** to worship Allah, my God. At the mosque, my family and I **pray**."

SHARING BELIEFS

Sharing our beliefs is an important part of our freedom. Having freedom means that we all have rights. A right is something we are allowed to have or do. We have the right to express ourselves and to practice our religion whenever we choose.

One of the ways that Hindus express their beliefs is at a special festival called Holi. Holi celebrates the beginning of spring, and is celebrated with singing, dancing, and throwing colorful powder at one another.

LEARNING FROM OTHERS

You can respect others' beliefs by asking questions to learn about them. When you ask questions, it is important to listen to the answers. Listening can help you learn what others are thinking and feeling. Listening to other people express their beliefs will also help you understand them.

Marya's classmates wondered why Marya wore a headscarf to school. They asked Marya to explain the reason why she wears it. They listened to Marya as she told them why she wears the special headscarf called a hijab.

"I wear a hijab because I believe it is a sign of respect to God."

CELEBRATING BELIEFS AT SCHOOL

At school we can learn all about different religions. If you ever have a question about another religion, you should ask your teacher. You can also ask a friend who follows that religion to explain their beliefs to you.

It is important that we respect other people's beliefs at school.

Sasha doesn't celebrate the Christian festival of **Easter**, but she made a card for her friend who does to help her celebrate and to show that she cares.

CELEBRATING BELIEFS AT HOME

We often share the same beliefs as our families. Our family members can teach us the values of their beliefs. They can also show us how to be accepting and respectful of other people's beliefs.

Nila's family is Hindu. She learns about Hindu traditions, such as worshiping gods and goddesses, from her parents.

Leigh celebrates the Jewish festival Hanukkah with her family. They sing songs and light special candles on a menorah. A menorah is a special candelabrum, or candle holder. This makes Leigh feel close to her family members as they celebrate together.

menorah

MAKING A DIFFERENCE

You can make a difference by learning about other religions and being respectful of everyone's beliefs. It will help you to be understanding toward those who have different beliefs than your own.

Think of someone in your life that has different beliefs than yours. Learn about their beliefs by asking these questions:

1. What do you believe?

2. Where is your place of worship?

3. Do you celebrate any special festivals?

4. Do you wear any special clothes?

5. Do you eat any special foods?

GLOSSARY

Christianity [kris-chee-AN-i-tee] A religion whose followers believe in the teachings of Jesus Christ

community [kuh-MYOO-ni-tee] A group of people who live, work, and play in a place

Easter [EE-ster] A Christian holiday that celebrates Jesus Christ

festivals [FES-tuh-vuh ls] Celebrations that include ceremonies and other events

freedom [FREE-duh m] Being allowed to do something

Hinduism [HIN-doo-iz-uh m] A diverse religion originating in India

Islam [is-LAHM] A religion whose followers believe in one God, Allah

Judaism [JOO-dee-iz-uh m] A religion developed by the Hebrew people, following one God and teachings of scripture

law [law] Rules made by government that a community has to follow

mosque [mosk] A Muslim place of worship

Muslim [MUHZ-lim] Relating to the religion of Islam or Muslim people

pray [prey] To offer praise and thanks to a God or object of worship

respect [ri-SPEKT] The act of giving something or someone the attention it deserves

traditions [truh-DISH-uh ns] Beliefs or practices that have been handed down over a long period of time

worship [WUR-ship] To show a feeling of respect toward a god or gods

INDEX